LANGDON
The History of an English Manor House

South side and walled garden 2007. Photo: Hovercam

Robin Blythe-Lord

Langdon Court is a Grade 2* listed manor house on the South Coast of Devon between Wembury and Down Thomas. It is built from a mixture of Wembury siltstones, sandstones and brick with details in granite all under a slate roof.

The house has undergone several radical rebuildings in the past but it is unique in that it has never been destroyed, bombed or in any way structurally damaged. The house we see today is substantially that of 1707.

The accompanying estate once covered over two thousand acres and encompassed all of the peninsula between the Yealm and Bovisand.

A Hotel since 1960 it has gone from strength to strength culminating in the award to the present owners of a fourth AA star and a second rosette.

This booklet is an abridged version of the definitive book 'The Story of Langdon Court' ISBN 978-0-9541562-1-3 by the same author.

Dedicated to Lesley, Zoë, Elys, Rosie, Talitha, Gareth, Bruce and Lulu

Second Edition ©2013 Robin Blythe-Lord NDD, ATD, ADAE
All photographs and artwork by the author unless otherwise attributed

Camelot, Amacre Drive, Plymouth PL9 9RJ, UK.
Tel: 01752 403321
eMail robin@ateliers.demon.co.uk

ISBN 978-0-9541562-4-4
EAN 9780954156244

CHRONOLOGY and CONTENTS

SOME FEATURES OF THE HOUSE

Scratched into a downstairs window.
Who was George Crann?

Langdon Court East side. Photo: Hovercam

THE SAXONS c1044 to 1086
HECA and GODA

Prior to the reigns of the Saxon kings, Edward and Harold, Langadona, Langedone or Langdon was held jointly by two Saxons, Heca, (or Heche) and Goda, who might be related by blood or marriage. The land is 'held' that is it remains the property of the Crown. While the holders can live and work on it for their benefit the Crown could repossess it should the holders fall from favour, rather a neat way of encouraging loyalty. Goda is Saxon woman's name that is also associated with the family of King Edward. Heca is possibly the same Saxon landowner who gave his name to Egg Buckland, or Heca's Bookland, in Plymouth. Bookland being land granted by special Royal Charter. Langdon is derived from Lang meaning Long, Don meaning Hill. Hence Long Hill.

THE NORMANS c1086 to 1100
BARON JUDICHAEL and SQUIRE WALDIN

In 1066 came the Norman invasion and by 1072 William, Duke of Normandy, had subdued the country, pronounced himself King William and reallocated parcels of land previously owned by Saxons, which must have gone down well. The Langdon estate became the property of the Norman Baron Judichael (also recorded as Juhel or Godhel) for his help in subduing Exeter. He let it to his Knight squire Waldin, no doubt also as a reward for services rendered. Just what happened to the previous Saxon landowners is not clear.

In 1086, as a piece of stocktaking and to value the land for future taxation to fund the raising of armies against perceived threats, King William commissioned The Domesday Book. Langdon's entry shows that Judichael is the owner, Waldin is a tenant, and that Hece and Goda were the previous tenants:

'Waldin holds LANGDON from Judichael. Heca [or Heche] held it in the days before King Edward and it paid geld for half a hide. There is land for 2 ploughs, which are there, with 1 slave, and 4 villains and 3

5

bordars, and 2 acres of meadow and 4 acres of pasture. Formerly, as now, worth 10s.

It is more than likely that there was a Saxon hall or house somewhere on the estate and quite possibly near to the present Langdon Court. Home and Barton farms are usually closely associated with a medieval manor house. In the case of Langdon if the manor house stood on the present Langdon site then it would have been between Barton Farm and Home Farm, so neatly forming the centre of the Lord's domain. However the position of Barton Farm has moved so it is not certain that the original manor house stood on the present site.

THE PIPARD FAMILY c1100 to 1349

Around 1100 the estate becomes the property of the Pipard family. There is evidence that the Pipard family lived at Langdon between 1154 and 1189 and it is known that Sir William Pipard was Lord of the Manor between 1199 and 1216. William's son Thomas Pipard died in 1283, Thomas' son William Pipard died in 1301 and William's son, also named and knighted Sir William Pipard and who died in 1349, was the last of the line.

There is a record of the Chancery of Inquisition following the death of Thomas Pipard in 1283 that shows of what the manor consisted.

'There was a court [either a meeting place for the manor court or the manor house itself] with a garden and curtillage worth ten shillings a year.....There was a mill on the manor, also worth ten shillings a year...A rabbit warren worth two shillings a year [possibly the Mewstone]...five acres of meadow worth 7s 6d a year'.

Three more acres of meadow than mentioned in both Domesday entries for Langdon. The estate is growing.

The 1332 Devonshire Lay Subsidy lists the tax paying farmers (villains) of Langdon as:

William Pipard 3s	[£67.15]
Walter de Tettecot 12d	[£22.38]
Nicholas Rogger 12d	[£22.38]
Richard Reymond 9d	[£16.79]
Richard Benet 9d	[£16.79]
Roger Cole 9d	[£16.79]
Henry Cole 8d	[£14.92]
Roger Moryng 8d	[£14.92]
Henry Burnard 8d	[£14.92]
Nicholas Batyn 8d	[£14.92]
Robert Pyk 8d	[£14.92]

Sir William Pipard would not have had to farm his own lands, his ten yeoman farmers would have undertaken this on a rota basis and the land would have been divided up into one or two acre strips. In 1838 there were still five of these strips surviving in the triangle of land formed by the roads and tracks around Langdon Barton Farm.

1347-48 the Black Death arrived in Devon but what effect it had at Langdon is not clear.

It was a somewhat arduous journey to Plympton Priory to worship and Manors often applied to build a chapel on their premises. There was no chapel at Langdon but there was one at the neighbouring manor of Down Thomas that may have been shared, so obviating the need for a private chapel at Langdon. Alternatively the nearby church of St. Werburgh on Wembury Point has existed in some form or another since Saxon times and has been used by various owners of the estate.

THE COURTENAYS 1349 to 1539

When William Pipard's son Sir William Pipard died in 1349 the manor passed into the ownership of the Courtenay family of Powderham. They were a very large and growing Devon family with a senior and junior branch but it is not thought that any of them were actually in residence at Langdon. It seems that Sir Philip Courtenay was probably involved with the Wars of the Roses for there is evidence that he granted power of attorney to William Rowse to act as his agent at Langdon and, in 1478, to 'deliver the house to Simon Cole'.

Henry VIII

THE CROWN 1539 to 1553

In 1539 Henry Courtenay, Earl of Exeter, was executed for an assumed act of treason that involved his family's relationship to Reginald Pole and allegiance to the White Rose Plantagenets. Henry VIII was aware that his own claim to the throne was not as strong as the Poles' and the Courtenays' and so was always suspicious that they were plotting against him. Many of the Courtenay family were either executed or imprisoned and the Langdon estate, together with all the other lands of the Courtenays, was forfeited to the Crown. It is not currently known who occupied the house at this time but it may well have been Simon Cole or his descendants or William Rouses' family.

At some time soon after 1539 a thirty year lease for Langdon was granted by the crown to John Wynslande, a lawyer of Furnival's Inn, London. This gave him an income from the estate and although his work kept him in London he may have visited occasionally.

In 1547, on Henry VIII's death, the house passed to Henry's widow, Catherine Parr. It is tempting to conjecture that she stayed there occasionally, however there is no evidence for this and we know that Catherine Parr moved to Sudely Castle in Gloucestershire where she married Thomas Seymour, brother

Mary Tudor

7

of Jane Seymour, and died shortly after giving birth to his daughter in 1548.

Henry was briefly succeeded by his 9yr old son Edward VI who contracted TB and died in 1553, succeeded by Mary Tudor. When Mary was entering London in triumph in 1553 she passed the Tower of London where four prisoners were kneeling to beg her pardon. One of these was Edward Courtenay who had been prisoner in the Tower for sixteen years, ever since the age of twelve when his father, Henry, Earl of Exeter, had been executed in 1539.

Edward Courtenay

Mary ordered his immediate release and over the next months developed an affection for him and restored his title and Langdon, amongst other estates.

THE COURTENAYS and THE CROWN...AGAIN
However Edward's romantic preferences lay with Queen Mary's half sister, Princess Elizabeth. All things considered not a bright move and a rather dangerous course to follow.

In 1554 Thomas Wyatt's failed rebellion occurred, Edward and Elizabeth were arrested on suspicion of being involved in the plot and sent to the Tower, after

Princess Elizabeth

all it was one of Wyatt's aims to put Elizabeth on the throne with Edward as her husband. Again Edward's lands, including Langdon, were forfeited to the Crown; one can see a sort of pattern emerging here... On the scaffold Wyatt declared that Elizabeth and Edward were not involved. Elizabeth was freed although Edward continued his imprisonment for two years after which he was released and allowed to travel on the continent. He was poisoned in Padua in 1556. The Earldom of Devon was not revived until 1831.

THE CALMADY FAMILY
In 1555 the Manor of Langdon was bought from the Crown by Vincent Calmady, an Attorney. In 1564 he and his brother Richard were granted full Manorial Rights by Queen Elizabeth 1st. An alternative version of this is that he was given the house 'for services to the Navy' though what these were, or could have been, is unclear but it is clear that he bought the manor.

The lease to John Wynslande may now have been terminated. Richard was later to exchange his share of the Langdon rights for some other holdings of Vincent's and so Vincent became sole lord of the manor. A contemporary description of the house was of it being 'complicated' and of 'medieval origin on a courtyard plan'.

Vincent was descended from the Calmadys of Poundstock, Cornwall. His parents were John and Frances Calmady who had five sons in all: John (the eldest), Richard, Vincent, Andrew and Edward. The Calmadys are a complex family with several lines and second marriages and marriage between cousins.

Vincent is often described as 'of Plympton St Mary' and for some years was resident at Boringdon Hall, then the property of the Mayhew family of Tavistock. He was an Attorney at Law and it seems that he was in the process of buying up parcels of land as they became available and he acquired portions of the manor land at Boringdon. He married twice. His first wife, Mary, bore him ten children, his second, Wilmot, three. The Calmady's were to become a large, influential and growing family with landowning interests over a wide area.

In 1562 a lease was granted to Vincent Calmady of Langdon by Sir Philip Champernowne to remove stone from the site of Plympton Priory for a period of 21 years at a cost of £1,207 which is equivalent to about £205,552.00 in 2009. The priory would have been in a pretty derelict state by then. The dissolution of the monasteries and the sale of their lands had resulted in one of the biggest property booms the country had seen. Everyone who wanted an estate, or the quality materials from one of the old buildings, was keen to buy.

Plympton had been the second richest monastery in Devon and Cornwall, exceeded only by Tavistock Abbey, so the building materials available were particularly fine. The first to have gone would have been the lead, then the glass, timbers and finally the stone.

Features of Plympton Priory, such as doorways and windows, can be seen incorporated into buildings in the area, such as the family seat of the Strodes, Newnham Park (now Old Newnham) in Plympton.

In 1565 Vincent's eldest son, Josias, was baptised at Plympton St Mary.

After 1565 it is difficult to pin down Vincent to a place. Often referred to as Vincent Calmady of Wembury but in a deed of 1577 he is called Vincent Calmady of Lewtrenchard. Around 1577 he started a substantial alteration to the house at Langdon, using the materials from Plympton Priory, particularly the three pillars in the main cellar.

Main cellar in Langdon Court

There does not appear to be any evidence that Vincent actually lived at Langdon Court on a permanent basis, however we know he was around there in 1569 though it seems that he mostly lived in his manor of Brixton, next door to Langdon, which would be reasonable considering all the building work being carried out at Langdon Court.

Vincent Calmady died in 1579. At the time his son Josias was a minor, aged 14, but would inherit the estate when he came of age.

In 1584 Josias married Katherine Courtenay, heiress of a younger branch of the Courtenays of Powderham and through her acquired the Leawood

approximately twenty acres in the Great New Park and the Deer Park to the north west. Between 1558 and 1603 we know the house was altered yet again, possibly to the classic Tudor E shape.

In 1611 Josias Calmady died aged 46 and Langdon passed to his eldest son Shilston Calmady, then 26, who was knighted in 1618.

There is a gap in the 1640's when Sir Shilston Calmady is listed as living at Leawood. Sir Shilston was a Roundhead

Langdon Court c1650. Artist unknown. Plymouth City Museum and Art Gallery. No remains of the tower on the hill have been found.

estate near Bridestowe in North Devon. Later he would inherit lands at Lewtrenchard from his uncle Andrew and estates of Farwood in Colyton from the death of his other uncle, Richard, MP for Plympton.

Josias and Katherine had one daughter and three sons.

At the latter end of the 1500's land enclosures began at Langdon. Josias, seeking to maximise his investment, removed the strip farming system and new park land was established,

supporter. Considering that he pledged his personal services to the Crown when he accepted his knighthood he must have been something of a disappointment to the King. The area around Langdon Court was staunchly Royalist with a post near the site of the present Fort Staddon and a substantial group at Hooe Barton Manor close by to the North. He evidently felt it advisable to stay at Leawood. At this time J. Rouse looked after Langdon Manor and was no doubt discrete regarding his employer's sympathies.

In January 1645 Sir Shilston Calmady was killed by a Royalist troupe in a skirmish near Ford House, Membury, North of Axminster nearly at the end of the Civil War. He was sixty years old and was probably visiting his cousins the Chases at Membury. On the 4th February he was buried in the chancel of St John the Baptist Church, Membury. Later his memorial was moved outside the chancel to the Yarty aisle. Langdon now passed to Josias, his heir by his second marriage to Honor.

The civil war ended in 1646 and Charles II came to the throne in 1660. The Calmadys' seem to have got through this period largely unscathed and Josias had commenced more renovation to Langdon by 1668, a date that is embossed on either side of the East door.

Josias died at Langdon in 1683 without issue. His will shows that the family had moved back to Langdon and his descendants settled there.

Josias' younger brother, Shilston of Leawood, succeeded to the Langdon title and married Elizabeth Gayer. They had three sons and two daughters. He died in 1688 after only five years as Lord of the Manor.

Shilston of Leawood's eldest son, Josias succeeded to the Langdon estate and married Elizabeth Waldo, daughter of Sir Edward Waldo.

Josias and Elizabeth substantially rebuilt the house again in 1707 and retained the existing cellars and their Plympton Priory pillars. This rebuilding was so extensive as to obliterate most of the previous Tudor building and took the form of the present rectangular William and Mary style house. Which might explain why the cellars only extend under the Southern side and half way along the West. At some time during this period the Calmadys' also created the renaissance walled garden that can still be enjoyed today.

Josias and Elizabeth had two sons, Shilston and Waldo. Both of these succeeded in turn to Langdon but both died without issue. So, following Waldo's death, the Langdon estate passed to the descendants of Francis Vincent Calmady who was the sixth son of Sir Shilston (he who was killed in the Civil War).

Francis Vincent had married Elizabeth Pollexfen, from the neighbouring Pollexfen family of Kitley. They had five children, Elizabeth Mary, Cecilia Anne, Francis John, Honor and Pollexfen. They used her mother's family name as her first name. When her brother Francis John died Pollexfen Calmady inherited Langdon.

In 1783, Pollexfen married her second husband, Admiral Charles Holmes Everitt. In 1788 he took the name and arms of Calmady by royal assent so ensuring continuance of the family name following the death of Captain Warwick Calmady, who was from another branch of the family.

Langdon Court 1821 by H W Bond

Charles and Pollexfen had three children: Charles (1788 - 1790), Charles Biggs and Arabella Phillippa. Charles died in 1807 and Langdon passed to Charles Biggs.

Charles Biggs Calmady married Emily Greenwood in 1816 and they had six children: Emily, Laura Anne, Vincent Pollexfen, Honora Mary, Cycill Christina and Gertrude Elizabeth.

By the time of the Tithe Apportionment of 1838 the Langdon estate had grown to almost 2000 acres and included, Court Barton Farm, Gabber Farm, Knighton Farm, Langdon Barton, Langdon Home Farm, Prince's Farm, Raneleigh Farm and West Wembury Farm.

The Calmady Children in 1823
L to R: Laura Anne and Emily.
painted by Thomas Lawrence.
Courtesy of the Metropolitan Museum
of Art, New York.

On January 1st 1855 Emily, Charles' wife, died age 61 and seven days later so did Charles Biggs Calmady. The closeness of their deaths would indicate a contagious illness of some sort, or maybe he died of a broken heart. They were both buried in Wembury Church. The Langdon estate now passed to their son Vincent Pollexfen Calmady.

For reasons that may be associated with estate duty Vincent Pollexfen Calmady put Langdon estate up for auction in 1872, after about 320 years in the Calmady family. It seems that it either did not sell or was withdrawn.

It was auctioned again on the 29th September 1876 and bought by Richard Cory, a wealthy ship owner and coal merchant from Wimbledon, London and the house entered a new and exciting period of its life.

Cycill Calmady c1875
Unknown Artist

Langdon Court 1876. Illustration from the sale details. P&WDRO

THE CORY FAMILY

On the 26th September 1876 Langdon Court Estate was sold to Richard Cory for £102,500. There is an apocryphal story that Richard paid for it in cash. At this time the estate comprised of 1,900 acres, had eight principal farms and 'various small occupations and various houses etc,' all of which gave an income of £3,000 pa.

The following year Richard began some modifications and additions to the building. The square embattled North West tower with hexagonal turret, the adjoining gateway to a small court over which appears 1877 RC; the chapel like single storied wing to the North West; the glazing of the central courtyard and probably the filling of the porch outer doorway and the insertion of a small rectangular one.

The Cory's are a large family that originates in Cornwall. William Cory (1783-1862) was born at Week St Mary in Cornwall, the son of a farmer.

He left Cornwall for London, sometime before 1810, to seek his fortune. He eventually founded a coal shipping and bunkering firm that was later known as Wm. Cory & Son Ltd. This enterprise laid the foundations for the

One of Cory's coalyards in Commercial Road, London. P&WDRO

family's fortunes and still exists as Cory Environmental. The original firm was in the coal trade with 13 wharves on the Thames, two floating derricks, leased depots in the Victoria, Albert and Tilbury docks, four tug bunkering stations, yards and works at Charlton, Erith, Brentford and Rochester, 2,500 railway wagons, 42 coal depots and 25 stables that housed the company's 350 horses.

'The Grove', Wimbledon. P&WDRO

William had a son: Richard Cory (1822 - 1904) who inherited the business. Initially he lived in London at 'The Grove', Wimbledon. When he was 54 he bought Langdon, using it as a country retreat, retirement home and shooting lodge.

Richard married twice, firstly in 1850 to Barbara Tinney, daughter of William Wallis Bray, and secondly in 1881 to Bessie Frances Coulthard, eldest daughter of Rev. T Coulthard of Plymstock.

Richard and Barbara's son, Richard Wallis Cory (1854-1926), was born in Bloomsbury and educated at Harrow and Exeter College Oxford gaining a BA in 1876 and an MA in 1880. He was called to the bar at Lincoln's Inn Fields but did not practise. He married Kate Rundle in 1882 and was JP for Devon and High Sheriff in 1910-11.

Mrs Bessie Cory 1902. P&WDRO

Richard Wallis Cory was on close terms with the Prince of Wales, later Edward VII, and knew of his female acquaintances, particularly the society beauty and actress Lilly Langtry. She did meet with him on several of his visits to Langdon, for the pheasant shooting, of course...

The Prince made several visits to Langdon Court in 1890/1902/03. He would arrive in Plymouth on a naval boat, transfer to a carriage and drive out to Langdon. It was not only the pheasant population that was put under strain by the Prince. His intake of food was prodigeous and would have made heavy demands upon the Langdon kitchen. For example his pre-shoot breakfast would often consist of haddock, poached eggs, bacon, chicken and woodcock. Luncheon was also substantial including very rich dishes

14

Shooting Party, Langdon Court. LtoR: Major Eden; Mr George Crake, (owner of the Tamar Brewery in Morice Town, Plymouth); Lord Monson; Son of General Way; Mrs Elizabeth Coulthard; Colonel George Gore; Richard Cory; Admiral Sir Alexander Buller; Mrs Bessie Cory; HRH the Prince of Wales; General Way; Major Hacket Thompson; Tim Hawkes; Captain Montgomery, c1890.
P&WDRO

such as game stuffed with Foie-Gras or truffles. He considered caviar and grilled oysters one of the best appetisers for a meal. At the time of his coronation his waist measured 48 inches, the same as his chest.

Evenings at Langdon consisted mainly of a large dinner, followed by card games, often baccarat (of which the Prince was particularly fond) or conversation about life in London, the latest automobile and the newly opened Tate Gallery. There was also billiards, reading from the extensive library, listening to the gramophone or the Organ (a colourful instrument 15ft high by 7ft wide with bellows worked by hydraulic power. Built in 1886 for Richard by Hele and Sons, Plymouth at an astonishing cost of £250, equivalent to about £12,000.

The Prince was very fond of practical jokes and a country house party such as at Langdon was often subjected to his pranks such as pieces of soap mixed with the cheese and a live cockerel put into the room of a sleeping guest. The entire party shared this form of humour. Perhaps they had to...

As well as shooting during the day the house could provide activities such as foxhunting, tennis and croquet on the newly created courts and lawns, walking, fishing, rides around the countryside in one of the carriages or just enjoying the splendid garden.

c1894-1895. On the garden steps. Lto R: Alice Phillips (step daughter of Archdeacon Wilkinson of Totnes); Bessie Florence Cory; 'Diney' Edith Frances Wright Cory; Edith Morton, (governess). P&WDRO

The children would be involved with many of these activities but had to maintain their education with their governess (of which there seemed to be a regular turnover) and it was very much a case of being seen and not heard. The Cory's were friendly with the Astor family who had a house on Plymouth Hoe, (3 Elliot Terrace, now the Lord Mayor's residence) and the children would play together and put on occasional theatrical performances.

The Corys were generally well liked and looked after their staff and tenant farmers very well. Robert Guyver in 1982 mentions that Miss Eileen Drake of Knighton, at that time one of Wembury's oldest residents, remembered Mrs Bessie Cory with great affection. 'Every Christmas there was present giving and rejoicing at Langdon Court when the tenants visited their landlords.' Richard was, according to his obituary in The Times, 'a good scholar and an excellent speaker but he had a strong dislike for public life, although he was prevailed upon to serve as High Sheriff of Devon in 1910 and was a county magistrate. He devoted himself almost entirely to the management of his large estate ... A fine shot and a keen fisherman he was nevertheless strongly opposed to hunting and would never allow hounds on his land.'

Circa 1925 the house was re-roofed with slate and it is possible that at this time the dormer windows on the East wing were removed.

Richard Wallis Cory died in 1926. It is said that in his later years his behaviour became increasingly erratic so he may have been suffering from Alzheimer's disease. He would wander off and the Head Butler had to go and find him. Soon after he died Bessie Cory rapidly married Colonel Gore. According to an apochryphal account from the time 'they had [allegedly] been doing a bit of courting for some time.'

Richard Wallis and Kate had a son, George Wallis Cory. Born in 1885 he eventually became a lieutenant in the 41st company, Royal Garrison Artillery that was stationed at Maker Barracks in Cornwall. In 1907 he died of pneumonia in Devonport Hospital at the age of 22. He had not married and Richard had no other sons so on his death the estate was put into the hands of his trustees.

FIRST AUCTION 1927

The estate is now in the hands of Richard Cory's executors, Kate Yolland Cory and George Tyrell Rundle who instruct that the estate is to be sold. It was split up into 65 lots for sale by auction on Thursday 29th September 1927 at the Royal Hotel, Plymouth, by Viner Carew & Co. and Fox & Sons (joint auctioneers).

The sale details show how the estate has grown under the Cory family and the modernisations made by

the Cory family. Coal fired (naturally!) central heating had been installed in the house and this heating was replicated in the gardens which had heated cold frames, nursery beds and greenhouses.

Beeston Boiler

The estate comprised of 2080 acres amongst which were Wembury Beach, the Mewstone, 14 fine dairy and rearing farms, the major portions of the villages of West Wembury, Knighton and Down Thomas, 2 fully licensed inns and 40 cottages and villas.

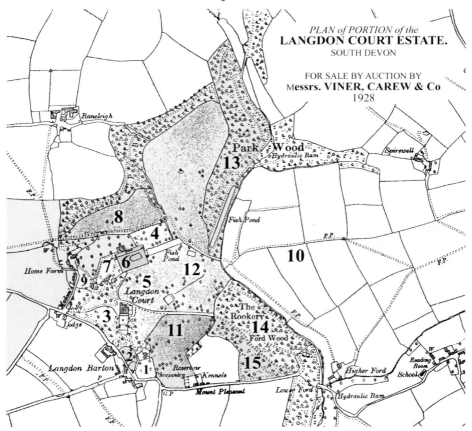

The land occupied by the current village of Wembury was sold from the estate as building land and houses were built here from around 1930 onwards.

However around 25 of the original 65 Lots remained unsold, including Lot 41 that contained Langdon Court, the highest bid for which was £12,000.

Above: West side, Below: South side 1927. Photos from the sale details

SECOND AUCTION 1928

The unsold lots were subdivided and Lot 41 became fifteen smaller lots. Another auction sale was organised for almost exactly a year later, again by Viner Carew, for Thursday 27th September 1928 at the Duke of Cornwall Hotel, Plymouth.

Langdon Court, together with other lots, were bought by Albert Edward Bechely Bechely-Crundall and conveyed to him on the settlement day of 12th November 1928.

Mrs GERALDINE KENYON-SLANEY

A conveyance document records that it was September 30th 1929 when Albert Edward Bechely Bechely-Crundall sold the property to Mrs. Kenyon-Slaney for £6,500.

What happened to the property in the intervening year is not clear. What little is known about A.E.B. Bechely-Crundall is that he was associated in some way with London & Home Counties Property Investments Ltd.

So, in 1929, Langdon Court is now the property of Mrs Geraldine Kenyon-Slaney. She is likely to have been in her mid fifties at the time and, as well as the house, she bought other Lots such as the walled gardens, Rookery Wood, all the fishponds, Orchard Cottage and the garage/stabling.

Geraldine Ellen Georgina Whitmore married Percy Robert Kenyon-Slaney (1861-1911) on the 23rd April 1893 and went to live in Santa Fe province, Argentina, where Percy had an estancia and bred polo ponies.

Their first two children, Philip and Frances, were born in Santa Fe province and baptised in the anglican church at Rosario.

After about 5 years the family returned to Percy's estate Langworthy, near Oakhampton, where they also bred Polo Ponies and had a Polo field. Here they had had two further children, Gerald and Stella. On Percy's death in 1911, at the comparatively young age of 50, Langworthy was inherited by the eldest son Philip.

Geraldine and the other children continued to live there while the children completed their education. In 1924 Philip was elected Unionist MP for Tavistock but his career as an MP was shortlived as he died on 9th September 1928, aged 32. Langworthy now passed to the eldest daughter Frances.

In the same year Gerald married Nanette Skipwith and Stella married Lt Col John Francis Barker-Hahlo KC, so 1928 was an eventful year for the family.

In 1929 Geraldine might have decided to move out of Langworthy and clear the house for her daughter. She discovered Langdon Court, fell in love with the place and purchased it from Becheley-Crundall.

Geraldine Kenyon-Slaney is recorded as being in residence at Langdon in 1930 and lived there continuously until 1938 treating it very much as a family home and becoming much involved with the local community.

In 1937 there were the rumblings of political unrest, the rise of fascism and the threat of war. Geraldine decided to put Langdon Court up for sale because she feared that, should war be declared, the house would be bombed by enemy aircraft heading for Plymouth Dockyard.

In September 1937 she started the sale process. The asking price was £6,500 or offer. The sale details show that the house had: '52 Acres of grounds. Hall. Billiards Room. 4 Reception Rooms. 15 Bed and Dressing Rooms. 3 Bathrooms. Water from private wells, Electric Light from its own generator. Central Heating. Telephone. Modern Septic Tank Drainage. Kitchen with an Aga cooker and a Beeston Boiler for hot water.'

She sold Langdon Court in 1939 to Eagle Oil and bought Waverley Hall, near Ashburton, Devon, where she died a few years later. In the event Langdon Court suffered no war damage.

Geraldine Kenyon-Slaney at Langdon Court, May 1935

L to R: Derek Barker-Hahlo, Stella Barker-Hahlo (Geraldine's daughter), Geraldine Kenyon-Slaney. Langdon Court walled garden 1936

South elevation 1936

19

EAGLE OIL

Eagle Oil bought Langdon Court from Mrs Kenyon-Slaney on the 19th October 1939 as office accommodation for their staff previously housed in Old Town Street, Plymouth.

The Eagle Oil and Shipping Co., London, was established before the first world war to ship oil from the Mexican oil fields to Europe. Their ships were involved in merchant convoys during both world wars. The firm was merged with the Shell International Petroleum Company in 1959 They were also mindful of being in a target area as war had been declared on September 3rd. and so were looking for accommodation away from imminent danger.

Geraldine Kenyon-Slaney put the house up for sale because she felt threatened, Eagle Oil bought it because they felt safer. A month after they had moved in the Ministry of Defence requisitioned part of the house.

MOD REQUISITION 1939-1945

The Army wanted Langdon Court as a safe HQ for Western Command, Coastal Artillery. This coincided with the establishment of the Cambridge Gunnery School at Wembury Point in 1940 for Army and Navy personnel.

Between 1940/41 they placed a single storey temporary prefabricated building over the East doorway and moved a mobile caravan onto the south driveway. If you look carefully around the current main entrance you can just see where the temporary building joined on. It is not entirely clear what happened to the Eagle Oil staff, whether they had to vacate the premises entirely or were allowed to share.

Photographs by an unknown member of MOD staff show that it wasn't a bad posting at all...

South side 1939

Croquet match 1941

Tennis players 1942

PLYMOUTH CITY COUNCIL

On the 25th February 1946 Langdon Court was bought by The Lord Mayor, Aldermen and Citizens of the City of Plymouth from Charles Pearce Brown and John Russell Baker of Eagle Oil for use as a children's convalescent home. In 1948 it was taken over by the National Health Service though still administered by Plymouth Special Hospitals Committee until 1958 when it closed. Improvements in home situations meant there was no longer a need for convalescent homes.

Langdon Court was intended for young children, typically aged 18 months to five years, recovering from illness or operation, and who came from very disadvantaged backgrounds mostly, but not exclusively, from the Plymouth area.

Where the child's natural home was very poor and would not be able to fully support the convalescence the recovering patient would be sent to Langdon Court. As one Nurse explained: "There was no question of 'you'll only be here for a couple of weeks or so' they stayed until they were fully fit."

Most of the time there were about 25 children but the number fluctuated between 11 and 38, all of whom slept in cots in a room on the first floor. Much of the house was unused.

The nursing staff consisted of Matron (Miss E Plum), Sister SRN, Two SEAN's, Four cadet or trainee nurses and two night orderlies.

The domestic staff: Cook, two kitchen maids, three domestics and a porter-gardener-handyman-stoker.

The MOD wooden building over the front door remained and was used as a play room. The Palm Court was where the children ate, supervised by the domestic staff. A previous patient remembers that it always seemed to smell of over cooked fish pie, peas and milky pudding.

Those children who were too young for school were taken for walks and down to the beach. There were also some pets and an aviary.

Parents were welcome to visit but required to notify Matron in advance. Without a car this would be a difficult place to get to. Small wonder that children could feel isolated and upset but the nursing staff did their best to make their time as happy as possible.

There was a rather critical report of 1956 that stated that Langdon Court had a rather too institutionalised regime and should try to make a more homely experience for the children. Things seem to have improved after that.

In 1958 it closed as a home and remained empty except for a caretaker and his family with occasional maintenance by a carpenter from Swilly Hospital in Plymouth.

Map of the estate as owned by the Ministry of Health and sold to Glenholt Ltd in 1960. This was essentially the same land as owned by Georgina Kenyon-Slaney and Eagle Oil. Map courtesy of Ordnance Survey

K G POWELL 1960-1964

Mr Kenneth Gordon Powell, known to family and friends as K.G., was the senior director and major shareholder of Glenholt Ltd., a country club and static caravan park 4 miles north of Plymouth beside Roborough Airport.

On January 29th 1960, while K.G. was away on business, the house was bought from the Minister of Health by two junior directors on behalf of Glenholt Ltd., for £9,000. It appears that they were thinking of converting it into a version of Glenholt. Maybe because of planning permission difficulties this did not occur but K.G. could see possibilities as a Public House with entertainment facilities and took over the project on behalf of Glenholt. He obtained the first ever licence for the premises and developed a turnover in the region of £10,000 a year.

In 1963 he took it out of Glenholt's ownership and created a separate company, Langdon Court Hotel Ltd., with himself as Director and his son, Chris, as Secretary. It is around this time that outline planning permission was granted for three blocks of bedrooms to be built at the top of the walled garden to create a Motel.

Firstly he built the present car park on the East side using stone from a field wall at Home Farm that the farmer did not want. With this he built the retaining wall and levelled up the hard standing, Once the car park was made he applied for a drinks licence and got the builders in. The morning room on the right of the East door as you enter was converted into the bar. Here the carved fireplace surround was taken out and moved to the opposite room, replacing the Adam style fireplace whose detailing had been badly damaged, possibly by convalescing children. A rustic stone fireplace with an open fire was created in the bar room. A bar counter, designed by Watneys' Brewery, was built across the left hand corner with a rear service counter and optics shelf against the wall.

The cellar was not used, instead beer kegs were kept in a nearby store now used for wine and rolled into the bar as needed. The room opposite the bar room across the hall was turned into a lounge and then a cocktail lounge with a small bar in the corner behind the door.

The most extensive work was on the East side of the first floor where the dividing walls between four bedrooms were removed, a sprung dance floor laid and a ballroom created with a small bar in what had been a dressing room at the North end to which all the kegs and bottles had to be carried. No work was done to create lettable bedrooms. As soon as the ballroom was ready wedding receptions were offered. There was a small stage in the middle in the alcove formed by the front door porch and this was used by live bands. At this stage the house was very much a pub with entertainment facilities but, according to the licensing application, there were plans to make accommodation for sixty guests.

Customers came from local residents, *HMS Cambridge* (the gunnery school at Wembury Point had been transferred to the Navy in 1956) and holiday makers from the nearby Churchwood Valley Estate of self catering chalets. The initial menu was rather limited but the cooking facilities were basic.

Squire's Supper: Rump steak, Onions, Tomatoes, Chips and Peas
Langdon Supper: Gammon steak, Onions, Tomatoes, Chips and Peas
Hunter's Supper: 16oz T.Bone steak, Onions, Tomatoes, Chips and Peas

The garden had gone to rack and ruin while the house had been closed and the Powell's spent a long time battling through the undergrowth. Inside the doors and other woodwork had all been covered with corporation brown paint and they removed layers upon layers of damaged Anaglypta paper.

Electricity was a continuing problem. The mains supply to the house was totally inadequate. Invariably it would cut off on a Friday or Saturday night blowing the mains fuse on the transformer box by the coachhouses. Electricity board engineers would have to be called to replace it. There was always a large supply of candles to hand as it was not unusual for Langdon

Court to be cast into darkness on a Friday or Saturday night, usually about half past nine. When this happened candles were lit on all the tables and the bar. The drill was to take one with you if you wanted to go to the loo.

K.G's son Chris did the day to day running of the hotel. Finding the hours very long and being offered a sales job with Tuborg Lager in Topsham, Chris decided to call it a day. K.G. agreed and the hotel was put up for sale in 1964.

Morning Room, 1960. Before conversion to the Bar.
Photo: Dermot P Fitzgerald

Palm Court 1960 before renovation.
Photo: Dermot P Fitzgerald

Bar after conversion. 1961
Photo: collection C&A Powell

Present Dining Room in 1960
Photo: Dermot P Fitzgerald

Car Park shortly after completion
1960. Photo: K. G. Powell

ALEC & JO MILNER. 1964 -1969

On May 8th 1964 Langdon Court was bought from K. G. Powell (Langdon Court Hotel Ltd.) by Alexander and Josephine Milner for a total of £22,780.12s.10d.

Alexander (Alec) Milner was a head brewer with various breweries in the Brighton area. Jo was a librarian and their son, Chris, was born in February 1942.

Around 1952 the family emigrated to Melbourne, Australia where Alec was under the impression that he would be working as a brewer for Carlton United Breweries. However there was no brewer's job and rather than return home he accepted the offer to be put in charge of a failing bottling plant which, despite his scanty knowledge of bottling plants, he turned around very successfully.

Further experience led him to be ultimately responsible for specifying, designing and running the world's first canning plant for Fosters Lager.

Jo was not happy in Australia so in 1959 they returned to the UK and bought the Talland Bay Hotel between Looe and Polperro in May 1960, for £10,000. This was in a poor state, complete with chickens in the front garden. They redecorated throughout and enlarged it by adding a front extension.

Four years later they sold Talland Bay and bought Langdon Court. Jo and Alec threw themselves into converting Langdon Court into a noteworthy country house hotel. They spent a lot of money renovating, redecorating, buying furnishings, designing menus, linen, china etc. The kitchen was expanded

and nine letting bedrooms created, decorated and furnished.

Mahogany tables and other furniture were bought from Beedell Coram Ltd. who were antique dealers in Plymouth. Arthur Negus was a frequent guest and used to run his hands approvingly over the furniture.

The coal fired central heating system did not work properly so they had night storage heaters installed, which proved to be a costly mistake, and the house completely rewired.

By all accounts Jo Milner was a perfectionist and the furnishings were of the best quality. It is also evident from the correspondence that she was the main driving force, Alec being content to run the alcoholic side.

It is testament to their hard work and dedication that they achieved, from ground zero, an AA/RAC two star rating, an entry in a good food guide and were Ashley Courtenay (Hotels Guide) recommended.

However Jo's health was failing because of the rigours of the work involved and, while the business could support the family, it would not support the addition of a manager.

In 1969 they put Langdon up for sale, and retired to Sussex.

Langdon Court China

25

DAVID and JOAN WAGSTAFF
1969-1979

In 1969 Langdon Court Hotel, land and buildings were bought by David and Joan Wagstaff, trading as the resurrected Langdon Court Hotel Ltd., for £19,000 plus an amount for fixtures, fittings and goodwill.

David and Joan were originally from Yorkshire where they owned four retail businesses. They sold those and moved to Hastings where they ran the White Rose Cafe. When Langdon Court came on the market it was an opportunity not to be missed. David ran the front-of-house and Joan doing everything else as needed. As David put it: "We were complete rookies at the time but we learned fast!"

They used the ballroom for a couple of years for wedding receptions and weekend dances, often to Maxie Rowland's Ballroom Orchestra. However the dances became too expensive to organise so they put the walls back where the original ones had been and returned the ballroom to four lettable bedrooms each with en-suite facilities. The ballroom floor still exists under the carpets.

They had to do a lot of alterations to comply with new fire regulations and put an additional bar in the lounge (now dining Room) opposite the main Bar, but took it out again after a short period. They put a solid ceiling under the glazed roof of the central courtyard to try and keep the heat in.

The gardens were very overgrown and they were not able to keep up with all the work these needed.

The property had mains water and electricity but the solid fuel stoves for

L to R: Harry Bone, Frank (Chef), Alec, Jo, Bill Butland, Langdon Court. 1964.
Photo: Chris Milner

The Regency Restaurant. 1964.
Now the main function room.
Photo: Jo Milner

South side 1964

Sale map 1969. Several fields have been sold off since 1964

cooking were taken out and replaced with Calor gas. The Electricity supply remained unreliable and they purchased a Lister diesel generator.

They had the 'secret tunnel' surveyed by Plymouth Polytechnic Caving Group and the well explored by RN divers. He converted the small cellar by the well to take the beer kegs and cooling equipment for the bar. An internal telephone system was installed for each bedroom

Ten years later, in 1979, David's health was showing signs of stress so he and Joan put the Hotel on the market and moved next door to the old coach house which they had already restored. They currently live in Down Thomas.

South front. c1970.
Photo: David Wagstaff

Dining Room c1970
Photo David Wagstaff

JOHN & SHEILA BARNES, ANN & ALAN COX 1979 - 2001

In 1979, the Hotel was sold to a partnership of John & Sheila Barnes and Alan & Ann Cox who had previously together owned the Headlands Hotel in Ifracombe and were looking for a place that would give them year round business.

The asking price was £195,000. John died, age 46, two years after purchasing the Hotel. They did a lot of redecorating, refurnishing and re-equipped the kitchen. Here the floor was relaid, a large extractor canopy fitted and new stoves purchased. They put a cocktail bar back in what is now the dining room and painted the moulding on the ceiling white on a blue ground. It became known as 'The Wedgwood Room'.

Important, but less glamorous, they updated the sewage system by installing a Klargister teatment works.

Reception was at the bottom of the main stairs, mainly because this was where the telephone lines came in. The main house exchange occupied a whole room by the kitchen stores. When this was updated in 1985 it became a small box on the desk and the exchange room had a walk in freezer installed.

The Marriage Act of 1994 allowed civil marriages to be performed in approved premises other than religious buildings. Langdon Court became a most sought after venue particularly with the work they did to improve the garden.

Day to day customers were coming from local residents, commercial bookings and, most importantly, *HMS Cambridge* who did not have enough accommodation for its own personnel and visiting engineers and so regularly used Langdon Court.

After twenty two years, and having become very well known and liked in the community, Alan, Ann and Sheila decided to retire to Heybrook Bay. As they say: "Times were changing and everything was getting very difficult. The staff employment regulations, fire regulations, all were more complicated and we all wanted to do other things. We had grandchildren and wanted to travel and do the things we had not been able to while tied to the hotel. It's a 24hr, 365days a year job really."

One of the factors that must have influenced their decision was the closure of *HMS Cambridge* in 2001.

Their last act just before selling was to remove the ceiling under the glass roof of the courtyard (now reception).

Reception at the foot of the main staircase. 1980. Photo: Alan Cox

L to R: Sheila Barnes, Alan and Ann Cox. 2007.

Above: The Wedgwood Room. c1980
Left: Small dining room c1982

28

MARK and RUTH JONES
2001 - 2007

In 2001 Langdon Court was bought by Mark and Ruth Jones for £670,000.

They met at catering college and their first job was at a pub, The Bell, at Horndon on Hill, Essex. Mark was the chef, Ruth a waitress. After six months they left to run a country house hotel in the Lake District for three years.

A move to Oxfordshire followed where they bought two pub/restaurants: The Angel at Long Crendon (which was sea food restaurant of the year 1977) from 1987-1997 then the Old Trout at Thame from 1997-2001.

When they first started at Langdon Court Mark was the chef and Ruth was front of house. There was an initial staff of ten which grew to thirty by 2007.

They removed the cocktail bar in the dining room and rebuilt the main bar. Replaced much of the plumbing, particularly the hot water system, replaced all the surface wiring with hidden wiring. The bedrooms and their en-suites were upgraded, those in the main bedrooms have walk in power showers and underfloor heating.

The glass roof over the courtyard was reglazed with clear glass in 2002 and repainted the supporting woodwork which was in excellent condition. Then reception was moved to the courtyard.

Many of the carpets and floor coverings were lifted to expose the original wood floors and tiles that Cory put in and a different, more muted, colour scheme used throughout.

A lot of weed trees in the garden were felled and this opened it up to views and walks. The slope down to the old croquet lawn was terraced and a flower garden created where the tennis court had been.

The old Pavilion was demolished as it had become rotten and dangerous. A great many daffodil bulbs were planted along the entrance drive, a wild flower meadow created on the facing hillside and they bought back a couple of the original paddocks.

The wedding business increased dramatically. When they took over the hotel they inherited twelve weddings for 2002 of which four cancelled because they did not like the new look, however another seventeen booked because they did like it; by 2007 they were doing a hundred plus.

After six years and feeling they needed a change they sold the Hotel and planned to return to the Lake District.

L to R: Aimee, Mark and Ruth Jones 2007

29

SW corner 2013

Reception Lounge 2013

House and Lake 2013

The bar 2013

Dining Room 2013

*Dartmoor Venison with Sauté Potatoes,
Celeriac, Beetroot and Blackberry Jus*

The Clarke Wedding

Premier Room 2013

GEOFFREY and EMMA EDE
2007 - present

Timothy, Emma, William & Geoffrey Ede. August 2007

Geoffrey and Emma Ede, with their two young sons Timothy and William and cat Boots arrived at Langdon Court in July 2007.

Geoffrey grew up in Australia with ancestors dating back to 1856, the previous ancestors are buried in Cornwall.

Emma's family background is in Canterbury, Kent. She is a university graduate who grew up in the service industry, as her family owned wine bars, pubs and hotels and is the strength behind the success of Langdon Court's growing wedding and function business.

Timothy and William now attend the grammar school in Devonport and feel settled and happy in Devon after attending King's Public School in Canterbury from the age of four.

Geoffrey's career started as a young ship's officer on cruise ships out of Australia bound for the Far East, the Pacific Islands and around the world service. After qualifying as Captain he returned to university in Australia where he studied for a Master's degree in business and moved into corporate life, managing fleets of ships around the Australian coast and the world.

He moved to England in the 90's to manage fast ferries and fleets to Scandinavia and New York that had been pioneered by Sea Containers, who at that time also owned Orient Express hotels and trains. Working for a company that owned the most famous train in the world and some of the world's greatest five star hotels inspired the purchase of Langdon Court.

Langdon Court has proved to be another challenge. As Geoffrey says: "Renovating a Grade 2 listed barn complex in Kent and a villa in Spain during the last seven years would not necessarily fully equip us for this task."

However, some two years and twenty skips later, a wholly new commercial kitchen installed by Allsop and Pitts, lights along the drive and around the house, new plantings, a lake complex and vineyard added, house renovated, new furnishings and a great team of staff... "we feel we have finally cracked the first stage towards making Langdon Court the best hotel and restaurant in Devon. The award of our fourth AA star and second rosette is an appreciated confirmation of our efforts."

South Side 2009

Function Room 2013

Tropical Fruit & Panacotta Bombe

Vineyard 2013

At Night. photo: Martyn Norsworthy

SOME FEATURES OF THE HOUSE

The Secret Tunnel

The entrance to the tunnel is in the East wall of the small South cellar/store.

It has been well built, cut through the stone bedrock and corbelled; running South East for about 73m and 4.6m below ground.

The main tunnel is filled in or collapsed at the far end, the roof getting lower and lower until the tunnel is impassable but a small pipe has been inserted at the end to drain the constant water that trickles through the passage.

It seems that the tunnel was broken into when Richard Cory built the tennis court and croquet lawn. Where it originally ended is not known.

About 25.9m along another smaller tunnel enters from the right. This smaller tunnel doubles back on the main tunnel changing to narrow rectangular shape and ends on a level with the main tunnel opening.

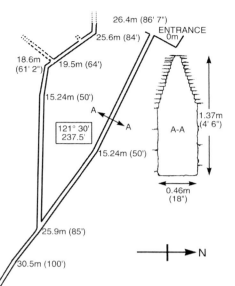

A rough survey on the ground above indicates that the spur tunnel lined up with the gardener's toilet on the East side of the garden wall with another spur to take the overflow from the fountain fed pond.

In May 1972 the Plymouth Polytechnic Caving Club carried out a survey and excavation. They found several coins, bits of pottery and pieces of glass some of which had either the Calmady seal on them or a trade seal that read 'Pyrmont Water'. It has been suggested that this was spa water from Bad Pyrmont in Western Germany and might be connected to Richard Cory's time as he was acquainted with Prince Wilhelm of Prussia who visited Langdon. Other finds included a doll's hairbrush, a small table knife and great deal of broken glass.

Passages such as this attract many romantic and fantastic theories of use. Being close to the sea, well smugglers are an obvious choice. Another is easy access to church and/or escape danger. The actual use may be far more prosaic, that of a culvert and drain.

The Saxon Well

Westerly Sundials

There are two Westerly sundials at either end of the West elevation. These only work after midday. Dated 1693 they are unusual in that they have the Calmady arms cut through the gnomon. They are 45mins slow as the house is not built on a true North/South alignment.

The well has been cut back into the bedrock to form a roof that has been dressed at the front with a barrel vault stone arch, the rest of the Well and the shaft being of rough hewn finish.

The top of the shaft is roughly rectangular, about 1 meter wide by 2.27 meters front to back and the shaft itself is about 10 meters deep cut into the bedrock with a slight swelling at the bottom. A vertical slab of stone about 45cms high has been positioned across the front at floor level. The water level stays at ground water level which is about 50 cms below the floor level of the cellars.

Calmady / Courtenay Arms

One of the main supporting walls of the house has ben built directly over it, indicating that the well predates the wall, which was built in Vincent Calmady's time.

The quartered arms of Josias Calmady and Catherine Courtenay, carved on a plaque over the original main entrance on the West elevation, commemorate their marriage in 1584

Stained Glass Window

The glass window on the half landing of the stairs was installed by Richard Cory before he glazed over the courtyard.

This is painted glass rather than 'stained' glass, the difference being that here the design is painted onto plain glass with fusible enamels. The glass is then fired to around 700°C which fuses the colour into the surface of the glass.

The scene is a romantic depiction of an Elizabethan episode. He could be Drake or Raleigh , she could be Elizabeth. The Houses in the background seem to be of Dutch origin.

The bags they are carrying are hawking bags in which a falconer would carry the meat tit bits to lure the bird back.

Despite the subject the window has been dated to around 1900. Judging by the style it is probably by Fouracre and Watson of Plymouth or Edward Frampton senior. It is not signed.

Fouracre and Watson had studios in Stonehouse, Plymouth and made windows for many local chuches. Cory was well known for his support of local business.

Edward Frampton was based in London. He was a Mason and made windows of a similar style for the Masonic boy's school at Clapham. Cory was a Mason and it is possible that this window was being taken out when the schol was sold and Cory obtained it.

It does seem that the window opening has been altered to accommodate it.

The following ground floor plans give a rough idea of how the house grew. With a house of this age, using a variety of building materials from a variety of sources and without documentary evidence it is not possible to be sure.

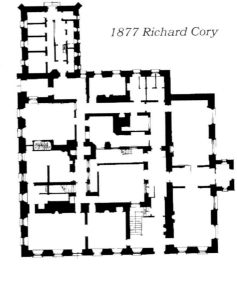

1877 Richard Cory

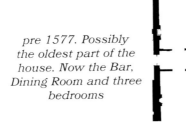

pre 1577. Possibly the oldest part of the house. Now the Bar, Dining Room and three bedrooms

1577. Vincent Calmady

1693/1707 Calmady

Tower Bellcote

At the top of Richard Cory's tower, hidden from the ground by the castellated wall around the top of the tower, is a charming bellcote constructed of granite on a local stone base.

Used for summoning the estate workers in case of emergency or marking the time. It was operated by a pull wire that hung down the outside of the tower.

THANKS TO:

John Andrews
Sal Axworthy
Carole Benney
Sheila Barnes
Zoë Bibby
Rex Booth
John Boulden MBE
Richard Cann
Nina Carder
Alan and Anne Cox
Joycelyn Day
Richard Dunn
Geoffrey and Emma Ede
Maurice Eglinton
Pauline English
Ian Frost
Marielyn Fryer
Jessie Greenstreet
Keith Hill
Gifford Hooper
Pippa Huelin
Michael Irwintazzar
Sofie Jackson
Ruth and Mark Jones
Anna Keast
Simon Kenyon-Slaney OBE
Maureen King
Mike Lyon
Peter Lugar

Duncan Matthews
Chris Milner
Chris and Anna Powell
Bill Savage
Gareth Skinner
Bill Tait
Thomasina Tarling
Graham Titchmarsh
David and Joan Wagstaff
Catherine Wills

British Museum
Companies House
Devon Local Studies Library, Exeter
Esse Cookers
Harrison and Harrison
Hele's Organ Builders, Saltash, Plymouth
Hovercam Ltd.
H M Land Registry
Metropolitan Museum of Art, New York
Plymouth and West Devon Record Office (P&WDRO)
Plymouth Local Studies Library
Plymouth City Museum and Art Gallery
South West Image Bank
Stained Glass Workshop

Langdon Court Hotel
Adams Lane
Down Thomas
Plymouth
Devon
PL9 0DY

Tel : 01752 862 358
Fax : 01752 863 428

Email : enquiries@langdoncourt.com
Web : www.langdoncourt.com

BIBLIOGRAPHY

1875 Langdon Court Sale Particulars, P&WDRO

Baptism Register, St Bartholomew's Anglican Church, Rosario, Argentina

Edward VII, Keith Middlemas, Wiedenfeld & Nicholson, 1972

Lecture notes to Plymstock Civic Society, Robert Guyver, 1982

Domesday Book, National Archives I/07/00946081P

Economic History Review, Mark Bailey, LI, 2(1998)~ pp. 223-251 *Peasant Welfare in England*, 1290-1348

The Romantic Story of Wembury Church, Rev. K Tagg, 1945 and 2nd. edition 1989

Wembury at the First Millenium, Edited by Michael B Arnold, Published by Wembury Local History Society, 2000

Plympton's Past in Pictures, John Boulden MBE, 2007

Recollections of Wembury, Arthur Clamp, 1995

A Pedigree of The Calmady Family, Laura Calmady 1304 - 1896 Unpublished, P&WDRO

The Book of Bridestowe: Gleanings of a Devonshire Parish (Community History Series), Richard Cann, Halsgrove, ISBN: 978-184114, 1961

Langdon Court, Alan D Cox, 1984. 3rd edition, 1988

A description of Langdon Court, G W Copeland, Unpublished, c1965.

Printed and bound by
Latimer Trend & Co, Plymouth